SCHOLASTIC

Reading Manga: What is it?

The Japanese word 'manga' has been used for nearly 200 years. It means whimsical pictures (man = whimsical, ga = pictures).

Today, manga is a label for Japanese-style graphic novels, comic books and animated movies (also called anime). What's the difference between a graphic novel and a comic book? The answer is in your hands. Graphic novels are usually quality productions, sometimes run to hundreds of pages, and often cover serious subjects. Many Japanese manga focus on topics like the environment, the law, science, history – you name it.

Manga don't all look exactly the same, but they have some things in common:

Big Eyes

Oversized Expressions

Fast Action

Reading Manga: How to Follow

Each page of a graphic novel is divided into boxes called panels. You follow the panels from left to right and top to bottom, like this:

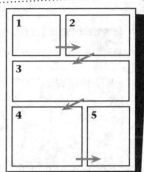

Each panel is like a paragraph in a regular book. It shows you where the characters are, and what they are doing, saying and thinking.

Some panels include a little box at the top (or the bottom), giving you information about what's going on. These are called captions.

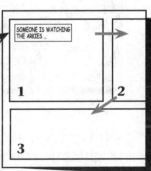

DID YOU KNOW?

Traditional Japanese manga look a little different. That's because in Japan, people read from right to left. Japanese manga is read like this:

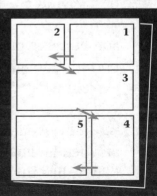

It's easier than it looks!

Reading manga: Who's talking?

Speech balloons tell you who is speaking, what they're saying, and how.

THIS IS A SPEECH BALLOON.

PSST. I'M WHISPERING. CAN YOU TELL?

THIS IS HOW I SHOUT!

NOW I'M THINKING.

Sometimes the lettering changes, to tell you which words are most important. These words might appear in **BOLD** or LARGE TYPE or in *ITALICS*.

Sometimes a punctuation point is enough to explain what's going on.

And how would you show an alien language? Maybe like this:

Reading Manga:
What's that sound?

When you read speech bubbles, you hear manga characters' voices inside your head. There's a way to hear the background noises too – the rumble of thunder, the ringing of a telephone, the crack of a stick underfoot.

Manga artists represent sound effects (or SFX) by placing words over the panels, using lettering to suit each particular sound. It looks like this:

Scary sound

Mechanical sound

Quiet sound

DID YOU KNOW?

Japanese manga SFX are very precise. For example, *bicha bicha* means small splash, *bashan* is a medium splash, and *zaban* is a very big splash. There's even a SFX for total silence: *shiin*.

SFX are used to show emotions as well. The word *unzori* placed next to a character tells you they're feeling bored. If it was *moji moji* they'd be feeling shy, and *shobo shobo* indicates sadness.

Reading Manga:
What's that look on your face?

Manga characters have exaggerated expressions, to help you understand what they're feeling. The first feature everyone notices is the eyes, which may be wide open in:

Shock

Fear

Hope

Closed eyes can mean:

Laughter

Sadness

Noses and chins are more difficult to spot (some characters have no nose at all). This reflects the Japanese preference for delicate features. In manga, big noses and chins are kept for the bad guys.

Reading Manga:

What's that look on your Face?

Just like manga characters' eyes, manga mouths are either huge or tiny. A big, wide-open mouth indicates:

Fear

Anger

Happiness

A character with a little mouth may be feeling:

Sad

Thoughtful

Shy

You can also tell a lot about manga characters from the crazy colour or style of their hair. For example, blue hair can mean the character is cool-headed, while orange hair equals determination (and sometimes a fiery temper). Wild, spiky hairstyles show the character is adventurous.

Characters

Perry

Perry tries to be sensible – he really does. But he can't say no to an adventure.

Fasool

Fasool is a hot-head. He often leads Perry into trouble – if Perry doesn't lead him there first.

Sergeant Zach

Perry's Uncle, he is one of the troopers who patrol *Spartan*. He tries (but fails) to keep the boys out of strife.

Other Folk

Diesel Halftone

A Spartan bully, known more for his muscles than his brain-power.

Professor Dunderbed

Perry and Fasool's biology teacher. He is even crazier than he looks…

SOME THINGS NEVER CHANGE. PERRY AND FASOOL ARE HARD AT WORK IN DETENTION.

I TOLD YOU TO KEEP YOUR VOICE DOWN. WHY DID YOU CALL PROFESSOR DUNDERBED A DUNDERHEAD?

IT JUST CAME OUT. BED AND HEAD RHYME. I CAN'T HELP IT IF I'M A POET.

FINALLY THE ANIMAL PEN IS ALL SHIPSHAPE.

OK, MATE. LET'S GET OUT OF HERE BEFORE IT GETS MESSY.

YEAH. YOU'D THINK BY NOW WE COULD BREED LIVESTOCK THAT DOESN'T DROP ITS MESS EVERYWHERE.

BIOLOGY CLASS!

RIGHT, BEFORE YOU GO, SWALLOW THE CONTENTS OF YOUR VIALS. THE NANOBOT TONIC WILL MAKE YOU ALL HEALTHY AND WISE.

IT'S A SHAME DUNDERHEAD DOESN'T TRY SOME. GRRRR.

RIGHT, AS IF IT'S GOING TO WORK ON DIESEL. HA!

BOTTOMS UP.

GUZZLE, GUZZLE.

OK, CADETS. GO STRAIGHT TO YOUR CABINS AND REMAIN THERE UNTIL THE 'ALL CLEAR' IS SOUNDED.

WHEN PERRY AND FASOOL REACH THE INFIRMARY THEY CAN'T BELIEVE THEIR EYES.

INFIRMARY

EEK!?

YIKES! EITHER WHAT YOU'VE GOT IS SPREADING TO THE FURNITURE OR I'M SEEING THINGS.

PERRY AND FASOOL DIVE FOR A DIAL-A-DESTINATION JUMP GATE, KNOWING IT COULD TAKE THEM ANYWHERE.

LOOK! A JUMP GATE. HOW LUCKY'S THAT?

YOU CALL THAT LUCK?! KNOWING OUR LUCK IT'LL PLONK US OUTSIDE SPARTAN WITH FIVE SECONDS OF AIR IN OUR LUNGS.

WHAT, YOU WANT TO LIVE FOREVER? YOU KNOW WHAT THEY SAY.

NO, WHAT DO THEY SAY?

DESPERATE TIMES CALL FOR DESPERATE MEASURES.

GOODBYE CRUEL WORLD.

WHOOSSSSSHHHH!!

THE BOYS HAVE BEEN TRANSPORTED TO ANOTHER SECTOR OF SPARTAN. BUT THEY ARE NOT ALONE...

MAYBE THESE THINGS ARE JUST AFTER YOU. I'M NOT GOING TO DESERT YOU, BUT...

DON'T EVEN THINK ABOUT IT, PERRY!

YIKES!?

DOES THAT ANSWER YOUR QUESTION?

THE BOYS HEAR A VOICE...

WHAT ARE YOU BOYS UP TO?

ARGH!?

DITTO!

- 20 -

YOU'RE SUCH A SCAREDY-CAT, FASOOL. ALL THESE ANIMALS ARE DEAD.

GRROWL

TRY TELLING THAT THING THAT IT'S DEAD! LOOK OUT!

GRROWL!

JUST LIKE THE FURNITURE, THE MUSEUM ANIMALS ARE ON THE MOVE!

CRIKEY. THAT WAS CLOSE.

SO IS THAT! WATCH OUT!

SAVE YOURSELF! TAKE THE LEFT AND I'LL TAKE THE RIGHT.

ARE YOU CRAZY? YOU THINK I'M GOING TO LET YOU HAVE ALL THE FUN!?

THE BOYS LEAP INTO AN AIRLOCK.

DID I TELL YOU PART OF MY PLAN IS TO FIND PROFESSOR DUNDERBED?

ER NO. YOU FORGOT THAT.

I DON'T WANT TO SCARE YOU BUT TIME'S RUNNING OUT.

DON'T I KNOW IT. I'M ALMOST COMPLETELY COVERED WITH THIS STUFF.

SECTION B

SECTION EIGHT. LET'S GET IN THERE!

GREAT. THE SECTION THAT'S CAUSED ALL OUR PROBLEMS AND WE'RE HEADING INTO IT...

DIESEL LAUGHS AS THE BOYS RACE PAST...

...BUT NOT FOR LONG.

SLAM!

A HOOK DRAGS THE BOYS THROUGH AN OPEN DOOR...

EEK!?

ARGH!

...AND THE TROOPERS RUSH PAST.

PROFESSOR DUNDERBED HAS SAVED THE BOYS.

!?

THIS IS MORE SERIOUS THAN I FIRST THOUGHT!

JUST WHAT WAS IN THAT NANOBOT HEALTH DRINK YOU GAVE US?

YEAH!

NANOBOTS, MY DEAR BOYS, NANOBOTS. BUT NOT NANOBOTS AS WE KNOW THEM.

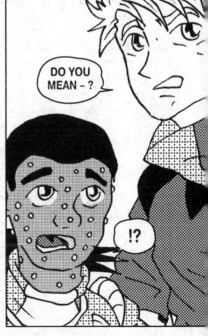

DO YOU MEAN - ?

!?

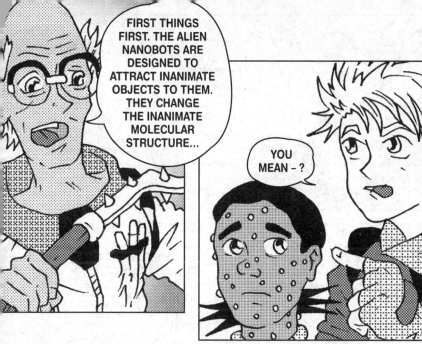

AH WELL, EASY COME EASY GO. I SAY, UNDER MORE CONTROLLED CONDITIONS WILL YOU BE MY GUINEA PIG AGAIN?

NO, I THOUGHT NOT.

WHAT I'D LIKE TO KNOW IS HOW FASOOL BECAME INFECTED IN THE FIRST PLACE!

IT WOULDN'T HAVE ANYTHING TO DO WITH DIESEL HALFTONE AND HIS FATHER WHO HAULED IN THAT SPACE WRECK, WOULD IT?

SPACE WRECK? WHAT SPACE WRECK? OH, THAT SPACE WRECK! WELL, YES... FANCY THAT. METAL THAT NANOBOTS BRING TO LIFE!

AND WAY TOO DANGEROUS TO RELEASE FROM QUARANTINE.

EXACTOMONDO.

SIGH.

SERGEANT ZACH FINDS THE BOYS. HE'S CAUGHT THE TROUBLEMAKERS, TOO.

UNCLE – I MEAN, SERGEANT ZACH!

THERE YOU ARE. IT'S SAFE TO COME OUT NOW.

AS FOR YOU TWO, YOU'VE GOT A LOT OF EXPLAINING TO DO.

BOY, IF THAT'S WHAT DRINKING A HEALTHY NANOBOT DRINK DOES TO YOU, I THINK I'LL GO WITHOUT IN FUTURE...

Cadets Junior members of *Spartan*'s military – like Perry and Fasool.

Dial-a-Destination jump gate A transmitter that shifts people or matter from one place to another.

Infirmary *Spartan*'s hospital.

Lockdown A command that means everyone has to return to their quarters.

Nanobotolia A disease spread by nanobots.

Nanobots Microscopic robotic devices.

Space wreck Craft that are no longer functional.

Spartan A huge space-faring ship.